DAVID SIL
MAGIC OF E

The Life and Career of One of the Greatest Midfielders of His Generation

JONATHAN JOHNSON

TABLE OF CONTENTS

INTRODUCTION

Following a knee injury, David Silva has announced his retirement from football.

The 37-year-old suffered anterior cruciate ligament damage while practicing with Real Sociedad, his current La Liga team.

He has now decided to end his stellar career, which spanned both Club and Country. He will be remembered as one of the greatest players in history.

Silva declared his retirement and said:

I am a fortunate man who has been able to pursue his passion, which is playing football, in the company of the best athletes, teammates, and friends.

While I am disappointed that I cannot support La Real during this thrilling season, I am glad for the experiences I have had over the years.

In my hometown of Arguineguin, where I first discovered my love for football, I've had several incredible experiences.

I started by enrolling in the Valencia academy at the age of 14, followed by lovely loans to Elbar and Vigo, and then by settling into Valencia's first squad and winning the Copa del Rey.

I then spent an incredible ten years at Manchester City. I had amazing success there, winning titles like Premier Leagues, FA Cups, and League Cups with a team that will always hold a special place in my heart.

Additionally, I consider myself extremely fortunate to have been a member of the greatest national squad in our country's history, which helped us win the World Cup and two European Championships.

Finally, I'll mention my arrival in San Sebastian, where I was treated like a member of the family. The team and the staff, just like when we won the Copa del Rey and qualified for the Champions League, I'm convinced, have what it takes to bring us excellent results.

I want to thank everyone who has supported me along the way, including my teammates, staff, and fans, before I say goodbye.

My family deserves special thanks because they have always been there for me in both good and—more importantly—bad times.

Without you, I never would have succeeded.

Many thanks for everything!

Chapter 1: The Magician

Early Life and Introduction to Football

David Silva was born in Arguineguin, Spain, on January 8, 1986. He was raised in a little town on the island of Gran Canaria, where he first developed a passion for football.

Silva's father, Fernando, encouraged his son to play football from an early age because he was an avid amateur player. Eva, David's mother, taught him the value of hard work and the will to succeed. Eva was of Japanese origin. Silva began his football career in the Maspalomas region with the UD San Fernando youth team. He began playing as a goalie before switching to the flank and modeling his style after Michael Laudrup, his childhood football hero.

He was allowed to join Valencia CF as a youth player when he was 14 years old, and he accepted. He lasted until he was 17 years old in Valencia's youth system.

Silva's early years in Valencia were challenging. He had a hard time adjusting to life in a big metropolis and felt homesick. He soon overcame these obstacles, though, and made a name for himself as one of Spain's most promising young musicians.

Silva earned his Valencia senior debut in 2004. He rapidly established himself as a team regular, and in 2008, he assisted the team in winning the Copa del Rey. He joined Manchester City in 2010 for a club-record £24 million transfer price.

One of his generation's most gifted midfielders is Silva. He is an excellent playmaker and dribbler with excellent game sense. He is a committed professional who works hard.

Silva faced hardships in his early years and when he first started playing football, but he overcame them to become one of the best players in the world. He serves as an example for young football players globally.

Silva's Abilities And Playing Style

Midfielder David Silva is a gifted passer, dribbler, and visionary who is bright and creative. Although he is a very adaptable player who can fill a range of roles, he is most effective as an attacking midfielder or winger.

Silva's passing skills are among his most amazing qualities. He can locate his teammates with pin-point accuracy even in confined situations because of his exceptional passing range. In addition, he excels at giving his teammates opportunities and has a talent for spotting open players.

Silva is an excellent dribbler as well. Both his precise control and balance allow him to evade defenders, while his speed allows him to outrun opponents. He frequently exploits his dribbling skills to open up opportunities for himself or his teammates because he is not hesitant to challenge defenders.

Silva also has a clear sense of the game's direction. He is always seeking opportunities to generate opportunities because he can spot passes that other players cannot.

He is also quite skilled at reading the game; he can predict where the ball will be before it appears.

Silva is a skilled passer, dribbler, and visionary player in addition to being a diligent worker and a committed professional. He is always willing to go above and above and is constantly trying to get better. He is also a great teammate who is constantly eager to assist his colleagues.

Silva is one of the most productive midfielders of his time due to his playing style and personal qualities. With Valencia and Manchester City, he has won many trophies, and he has also played a significant role for Spain's national team. He will go down in history as one of the greatest midfielders to ever play the position since he is a true legend of the sport.

His Commitment And Work Ethic

David Silva is a committed professional who works very hard. He is always willing to go above and above and is constantly trying to get better. He is also quite skilled at reading the game; he can predict where the ball will be before it appears.

One of the reasons Silva has been so successful during his career is his strong work ethic. He is always willing to put in the extra effort, and he is constantly trying to get better. Because of this, he is a very significant asset to any team, which is one of the reasons he has had such a great career.

Here are some instances of Silva's perseverance and work ethic:

He has a reputation for showing up early for training and staying late. He is always enhancing his technique and physical condition. He's always trying to find methods to get better.

Silva's desire to pick up new skills from other people demonstrates his commitment to his craft. He never stops trying to get better and never hesitates to approach teammates or coaches for advice. He is very coachable as a result, which is one of the reasons he has been able to adjust to many playing styles throughout his career.

Two of the qualities that make Silva such a unique player are his work ethic and passion.

Chapter 2: The Winner

David Silva's Trophy Cabinets

Here are some of the awards David Silva has received during his career:

UEFA Euro 2008: Silva's goal in the championship game against Germany was crucial to Spain's win at the 2008 UEFA European Championship.

The Spain team that triumphed in the 2010 FIFA World Cup in South Africa included Silva. Against Honduras in the group stage, he scored a goal.

Silva won his second UEFA European Championship in 2012 after scoring against Italy in the championship match.

Silva won four Premier League championships with Manchester City in the years 2011–12, 2013–14, 2017–18, and 2018–19.

Silva won two FA Cups with Manchester City, one in 2011 and the other in 2019.

With Manchester City, Silva won five League Cups in 2014, 2016, 2018, 2019, and 2020.

Silva won three Community Shields while playing for Manchester City, in 2012, 2018, and 2019.

His Contribution to Manchester City's Achievement

Over the past ten years, David Silva has been a crucial part of Manchester City's success. He was a key member of the team and assisted them in winning four Premier League championships, two FA Cups, and five League Cups.

Silva was a talented and perceptive midfielder who could dictate play through his passes and vision. He was a great dribbler as well and was not hesitant to challenge defenders. Because of this, he was an extremely dangerous player and a constant goal threat.

Silva was a great teammate who was always eager to assist his colleagues.

On the field, he was a leader who always led by example for his teammates.

It is impossible to overestimate Silva's contribution to Manchester City's success. He was a key member of the team and contributed significantly to their success. He will be regarded as one of Manchester City's all-time greatest players.

The following are some of the ways Silva helped Manchester City succeed:

A crucial playmaker, Silva was always able to find his teammates with his passing. He was one of the Premier League's most inventive players. He gave his teammates innumerable opportunities, and he played a significant role in Manchester City's offensive prowess.

Silva worked hard and was always seeking ways to get better. He was always eager to put in the extra effort. He was a consummate professional who established a high standard for his colleagues.

He was a leader: Silva was always a role model for his teammates and a natural leader on the field. He will be regarded as one of the best players to have ever represented the club because he was a vital part of the Manchester City squad that won the Premier League four times.

Silva's contribution to Manchester City's triumph cannot be disputed. He was a key member of the team and contributed significantly to their success. He will be regarded as one of Manchester City's all-time greatest players.

His Contributions to Spain's National Team

Over a decade ago, David Silva played a significant role in the Spanish national team. He was a member of the squad that won the 2010 FIFA World Cup, the 2008 UEFA European Championship, and the 2012 UEFA European Championship.

Silva was a talented and perceptive midfielder who had the ability to dictate play through his passes and vision. He was a great dribbler as well and was not hesitant to challenge defenders. Because of this, he was an extremely dangerous player and a constant goal threat.

It is impossible to overestimate Silva's achievements for the Spanish national team.

He was a key member of the team and contributed significantly to their success. He will be regarded as one of Spain's all-time greatest players.

Silva's contribution to the success of Spain's national squad cannot be disputed. He was a key member of the team and contributed significantly to their success. He will be regarded as one of Spain's all-time greatest players.

His Individual Awards

Silva has earned numerous solo honors in addition to these team trophies, such as the following:

PFA Young Player of the Year: In 2010, Silva was named the PFA Young Player of the Year.

PFA Team of the Year: In 2010–11, 2011–12, and 2017–18, Silva was named to the PFA Team of the Year three times.

Footballer of the Year in the FWA: Silva received this honor in 2012.

One of the most decorated footballers in Spanish history is Silva. He is regarded as one of the best midfielders of his time and has won many awards at both the club and international levels.

Chapter 3: The Leader

Silva's Captaincy of Manchester City

From 2017 to 2020, David Silva served as Manchester City's captain. On the field, he was a natural leader who always set a good example for his colleagues. He will be recognized as one of the best captains to play for the club because he was a vital part of the Manchester City team that won the Premier League four times.

Silva maintained his composure under pressure and was a very cool player. He was always able to maintain composure and make wise choices. Additionally, he was an excellent communicator and consistently succeeded in making his views clear to his teammates.

In the Manchester City locker room, Silva was a highly well-liked and well-respected member of the club. The younger players looked up to him and he was always prepared to lend a hand.

Silva led Manchester City with distinction as their captain. He was an important contributor to the team's success and helped them win four Premier League championships. He will be regarded as one of the greatest club captains in club history.

As captain of Manchester City, Silva made the following contributions:

He was a relieving presence since Silva was a player who remained cool under pressure. He was always able to maintain composure and make wise choices.

The team benefited greatly from this since it kept everyone motivated and focused.

Silva was an excellent communicator who consistently succeeded in making his views clear to his teammates. This was crucial since it ensured that everyone was on the same page and that the team was functioning as a unit.

He served as an example to his colleagues, and Silva was a well-liked presence in the Manchester City locker room. The younger players looked up to him and he was always prepared to lend a hand. The team's performance benefited from the pleasant and encouraging atmosphere this contributed to in the locker room.

Silva led Manchester City with distinction as their captain.

He was an important contributor to the team's success and helped them win four Premier League championships. He will be regarded as one of the greatest club captains in club history.

His Role As A Mentor To Younger Players

At Manchester City, David Silva was a very involved mentor to young players. He was always available to provide them with advice and assistance, and he was always prepared to assist them. He was a great addition to the team and played a key role in the growth of several young players into elite footballers.

The following are some of the methods Silva guided young athletes:

Silva was always prepared to assist younger players, whether it was by offering guidance on the practice field or simply by being there to listen. He was always kind and patient, and he never hesitated to devote his own time and energy to making things better for them.

Silva served as an example for younger players, both on and off the field. He demonstrated to them the value of professionalism, rigorous training, and winning attitudes. He was also a very modest individual who was always eager to impart his wisdom.

Silva achieved success. He was successful. He had achieved success by collecting awards at the club and international levels. This inspired the younger players and fostered a winning attitude.

Silva was a tremendous asset to the younger players as a mentor. One of the best mentors in Manchester City's history, he assisted in the development of numerous young youngsters into elite footballers.

Following are some comments made by young athletes regarding Silva's mentoring:

"David Silva has been an incredible mentor to me, " says Phil Foden. He has always been available to assist me and has taught me a great deal about the game. Much appreciation for your help".

"David Silva is a legend of the game, and he's been a fantastic mentor to me," says Bernardo Silva. He's given me a lot of gaming knowledge and improved my skills tremendously. Much appreciation for your help".

"David Silva is a wonderful gentleman, and he has been a terrific mentor to me, " says Riyad Mahrez. He has always been available to assist me and has taught me a great deal about the game. Much appreciation for your help".

Numerous young players have been impacted positively by Silva's guidance. He has mentored them as they grow into elite football players and instilled in them the virtues of perseverance, commitment, and humility. He will be regarded as one of Manchester City's greatest mentors in the organization's history.

His Effects On The City of Manchester

During his tenure at Manchester City, David Silva made a big difference in the city of Manchester. Fans of the city adored him, and he never shied away from supporting the neighborhood.

The following are some of the ways Silva changed Manchester:

Silva served as an inspiration to many young people in Manchester. No matter where they came from, he demonstrated to them that it was possible to realize their aspirations. Additionally, he had a very humble demeanor and was always eager to help others.

He was a generous individual who gave money to numerous charities in Manchester. Silva was a philanthropist. Additionally, he contributed to the awareness-building process for vital issues like homelessness and mental health.

He represented Manchester as a cultural ambassador by being Silva. He contributed to highlighting the city's multiculturalism and thriving culture. He was also highly well-liked by the citizens of the city, and he played a part in drawing tourists from all over the world.

The city of Manchester was greatly impacted by Silva. Fans of the city adored him, and he never shied away from supporting the neighborhood.

He will be regarded as one of the most significant individuals in modern Manchester history.

Here are some comments made by Manchester City supporters regarding Silva's influence on the city:

David Silva is not only a legend of the game, but also of Manchester. Both on and off the field, he has contributed much to the city. He was a true gentleman, and his absence will be felt.

David Silva is not only a spectacular footballer, but also a unique individual. He has consistently supported his followers and shown a willingness to give back to the neighborhood. He is a real role model, and we will miss him.

"David Silva is a legend in Manchester. He has made us all proud and has contributed to putting the city on the map. He is a genuine legend who will live on in memory for a very long time".

The city of Manchester was greatly impacted by Silva. Fans of the city adored him, and he never shied away from supporting the neighborhood. He will be regarded as one of the most significant individuals in modern Manchester history.

Chapter 4: The Man

Silva's Personal Life

David Silva is a highly quiet individual who rarely discusses his personal affairs. It is known, however, that he is wed to Yessica Suarez Gonzalez and that the couple has two children.

Yessica, Silva's wife, is a Spanish model and businessperson. When they were both youths, they first connected in Valencia, Spain. Mateo and Maria are their two children, and they were married in 2009.

Silva is a very devoted husband and father who enjoys spending time with his family. Vincent Kompany, a former colleague of his at Manchester City, is also a personal buddy of his.

Silva is an extremely modest man who dislikes discussing his affairs. He is a well-known kind and generous person, nevertheless. He is a role model for many young people because of his constant willingness to lend a hand.

His Charity Efforts

David Silva is an extremely altruistic individual. He has given money to numerous Manchester-area charities and worked to increase awareness of vital issues including homelessness and mental health.

The following are some of the charities David Silva has backed:

Manchester City's official charity is called "City in the Community."

Through sport and education, it seeks to improve the quality of life for Manchester residents. Silva has given money to the City in the Community and worked to increase awareness of the organization.

The Christie Hospital is a cancer hospital located near Manchester. Silva has made financial contributions to The Christie Hospital and has also met with patients there.

The NSPCC is a children's charity that seeks to safeguard kids from harm. Silva has contributed money to The NSPCC and worked to increase public awareness of the organization.

Silva is an extremely compassionate and giving guy. He is a role model for many young people because of his constant willingness to lend a hand.

His altruistic efforts serve as an example for all of us.

Here are some additional ways David Silva has contributed to humanitarian causes:

He has taken part in charitable games and activities.

He has given his time to charities and children's hospitals.

He has promoted significant issues using his platform as a football player.

Silva's humanitarian efforts serve as an example to us all. He serves as a role model for many young people and demonstrates to us that we can change the world.

His Legacy

David Silva is regarded as a sports legend. He is one of the most prestigious footballers in Spanish history and has received awards both at the club and international levels. He is also really humble and always prepared to lend a hand.

The legacy of Silva will live on for a very long time. He played a significant role in Manchester City's success over the previous ten years, contributing to their four Premier League championships, two FA Cups, and five League Cup victories. The Spanish national squad that won the 2010 FIFA World Cup and the 2012 UEFA European Championship had him as a crucial player.

Silva was a unique athlete. He was a gifted and perceptive midfielder with the passing and vision to dictate play. He was a great dribbler as well and was not hesitant to challenge defenders. Because of this, he was an extremely dangerous player and a constant goal threat.

Silva was a great teammate who was always eager to assist his colleagues. On the field, he was a leader who always led by example for his teammates.

The legacy of Silva will live on for a very long time. He was an exceptional player who excelled at the game. He serves as an example for many young people and will go down in history as one of the greatest midfielders to ever play the position.

The legacy of Silva will live on for a very long time. He was an exceptional player who excelled at the game. He serves as an example for many young people and will go down in history as one of the greatest midfielders to ever play the position.

Printed in Great Britain
by Amazon

37258550R00030